BURN

PITT POETRY SERIES

NANCY KRYGOWSKI AND JEFFREY MCDANIEL, EDITORS

BARBARA HAMBY

UNIVERSITY OF PITTSBURGH PRESS

Published by the University of Pittsburgh Press, Pittsburgh, Pa., 15260

Manufactured in the United States of America
Printed on acid-free paper
10 9 8 7 6 5 4 3 2 1

ISBN 13: 978-0-8229-6752-1
ISBN 10: 0-8229-6752-9

Cover art: Stuart Riordan, *Your Baby Ain't Sweet Like Mine*
Cover design: Melissa Dias-Mandoly

Publisher: University of Pittsburgh Press, 7500 Thomas Blvd., 4th floor, Pittsburgh, PA 15260, United States, www.upittpress.org

EU Authorized Representative: Easy Access System Europe, Mustamäe tee 50, 10621 Tallinn, Estonia, gpsr.requests@easproject.com

In memory of Stuart Riordan
and her sublime translation
of the human body to canvas and paper
and to our many years of friendship,
collaboration, and talks
about poetry and painting.
I will always miss
your giddy light in the world.

Eternal Aphrodite of the shimmering mind,
     daughter of Zeus, weaver of snares, Goddess,
don't break my heart, but come to me
     if ever before you heard my prayers and flew
from your father's golden palace on a chariot
     drawn by beautiful swift sparrows over the dark
earth, their wings beating from heaven
     through the air until you were here with me

-SAPPHO, ODE TO APHRODITE
(LATE SEVENTH CENTURY, EARLY SIXTH CENTURY BCE)

In the depths of winter, sit by the fire
     with a good bottle of wine.
Leave the rest to the gods.

-HORACE, ODE 1.9 (23 BCE)

CONTENTS

I.

II.

III.

BURN

Lady Brush Fire burns the high steppe, Lady of Raging
Battles batters everything into submission.
She, in the midst of havoc, shouting over the din
begins her sacred song, the song drawn
with a wand that carves her scheme for the universe.

-ENHEDUANNA, ODE TO INANNA (2300 BCE)

Night waits for us all.

-HORACE, ODE 1.28 (23 BCE)

Ode on Luck

What was I thinking when I got into cars with boys
      I hardly knew and drove to houses out in the country,
where my screams would be muffled by the oaks and pines
      and the teeming carpet of mushrooms, too stupid to know
I wasn't even close to being free, though I thought I was,
      but all that happened was we listened to *Blood on the Tracks*
and tried to write down lyrics in the flittering of candles, and
      I was dropped off at my apartment all too alive
to the possibilities of mayhem. Where was I going when I walked
      down the streets in my armor of beauty and youth,
lying in the sun, and thinking of Anaïs Nin in Paris, Rimbaud
      in Abyssinia, Kafka in Prague? How did I translate
my dreams into Italian? Not by planning, that's for sure,
      because I had no plans unless you could call reading
a plan, or daydreaming a plan, or making soup a plan,
      so if I could ask Lady Luck, what was the secret
to wooing her, she might say not giving a fig was a big part
      of it, also being happy with a stack of books
and infinite cups of tea or watching all those bummer foreign
      films like *The Marriage of Maria Braun* and *Last Year
at Marienbad,* throwing the tarot a hundred million times
      to see what was going to happen in the future
when it was going to happen anyway, or visiting psychics,
      who were canny in the extreme, figuring out
pretty quickly that when they told me I was going to have
      two, three, six children the look on my face
told them that this was not my dream come true,
      though there was that one in Houston who said
that in a few days I was going to have someone scream at me
      but not to get involved because I had nothing to do

with what was going on, and a few days later that's what
         happened—one of my best students started screaming
at me but it was because her mother was trying to take
         her daughter from her, and I was a great stand in,
maybe looked like her mother, so that was a piece of luck—
         me being tipped off by the psychic, and Deborah
having someone to yell at, i.e. me, her poetry mom, who
         in no way wanted her daughter, and I've had my share
of mommies saying snarky things to me on this same subject,
         because they had no idea how much work children are
even though they are adorable, but being the oldest in a big family,
         I knew, so that, too, was a piece of luck, though when I was
changing my little brother's diaper, it didn't really look
         like it, but that's the thing about Lady Luck,
she can show up dressed in rags, smoking a corncob pipe,
         and reappear twenty years later looking like Glinda
in *The Wizard of Oz,* it being a matter of interpreting
         your own life to yourself, which is what I'm doing
every day—translating my own language into an English
         that drives a spear into my heart, and I'll tell you
who's lucky—everybody and nobody in the same milkshake;
         you put in a scoop of chocolate, a scoop of raspberry-
dishwater sorbet, a squirt of kerosene, and lo and behold,
         there's a cherry, and what can you do but put it on top.

Ode to All My Late-Night Great Ideas

The Germans have a word for you—*Schnappsidee*—an idea
          fueled by Margaritas or shots of tequila or bottles of red
wine or white, you know the ideas that maybe involve a road trip
          to Miami or California and you wake up in a parking lot
in Mississippi or Delray Beach with a dead French fry stuck
          to the side of your face or you decide to drive over
to your ex's house at 3 am and give him what your mother
          used to call "a piece of your mind," and if you're lucky
you won't remember that psychedelic trip into the night
          or you'll be able to retrieve the piece of your mind
from the sidewalk where he either threw it or you fumbled,
          and it almost slid into the gutter, or what about the time
you volunteered to serve Thanksgiving to the homeless
          and all the women with their sliding makeup and soft
chins whispered, "We could trade places with you tomorrow,"
          or was that the Buddha, trailing along on the comet tail
of all the acid trips you took when you were sixteen, especially
          the night you discovered Motown, because you're slinging hash
in the 24-hour diner of your soul, and what is it that keeps you going
          through that dark night but four men singing harmony,
and so what if you end up on the side of the road in Arkansas
          reading a beat-up copy of *A Season in Hell* or *Fleurs du Mal,*
you still have "It Was Just My Imagination" flowing through your
          cerebral cortex along with Billie Holiday and Janis Joplin,
and that road trip across country in the 1966 Cadillac convertible
          with the boyfriend who hated to travel. Was he the one
you gave a piece of your mind to? No, that was another one who had
          so many rules about food that when you were behind
his new girlfriend at the local co-op and saw the belt full of tofu,
          lentils, soy sauce, turmeric, fenugreek tea—all the brown

meals you ate with him passed before your eyes, and you felt such a sense
        of relief that his Nazi regime was over, Berlin bombed
and you walking through the rubble, glad that you still had your arms
        and legs, but back to that Cadillac convertible on the road
from California to the East Coast, hitting Taos and trying to conjure up
        D. H. Lawrence and thinking about the description of Gundrun's
and Ursula's stockings at the beginning of *Women in Love,* but really
        we were driving to a one-month meditation retreat,
which is kind of the opposite of a car trip, sitting for an hour at a time
        and then walking and sitting and walking while your mind roams
like a wild monkey on amphetamines, but after a week in Himalayan
        storms, being attacked by pterodactyls swooping out
of the wild skies, you finally coast down to the plains or savannahs
        with their endless vistas of nothing and its brother and sister,
which is an oasis of cool water, and you find that your mind's zoo
        has lost its savage beasts, the lions now little pussy cats
and the wild boars, piglets, and yeah, it's kind of boring, but it's also
        like a radio with Bach playing, so you can always tune
into the Kinks if you need to, and I don't really want to tame my mind,
        but I do want to get the good out of it, leaving room for a riot
or two, though it takes so long to get over the riots—windows broken,
        walls collapsed, doors splintered—that you think, Is it worth it?
and I guess I'd have to answer, yes, the bombs exploding like fireworks,
        the shelves looted, and the little girls crying on the street
corner—Oh, that's me sitting with my torn dress and skinned knees,
        so please, Mr. Postman, keep all my great ideas in cosmic envelopes
and bring them to me whenever I need to be shoved out the door with no
        idea where I'm going or how or where the hell I'll end up.

Ode on Consciousness, Cell phones, Joshua Bell, and the Night of the World

Joshua Bell is sawing away on his four-hundred-year-old-
       four-million-dollar Stradivarius, and Grieg's Violin
Sonata No. 2 in D major is swirling around my head
       and invading my brain, the citadels of cortex
and nerve endings falling to the battalions of notes searing
       the room, when a woman on the second row
raises her cell phone, and for ten seconds I'm watching
       Bell play and watching his image at the same time,
and I can't help but ask myself which one is real—one is small,
       but other than that, he is the same—and isn't the man
on the stage a picture in my brain, much as the video
       on the camera, which is a little sharper than the image
on my retina, and how does something exist outside my mind
       and inside at the same time, not to mention the music,
which was born in the mind and fingers of a man in Norway
       and then a boy, who practiced hours every day
to be here with his ego and the pianist who played his scales
       and arpeggios, too, as well as the architect
of the concert hall and the team who installed the heat,
       because I lived in Hawai'i as a girl so even Florida
is arctic in February, but I'm warm, and before the concert
       I drank a glass of Sancerre, actually two, and they
are tamping down my inner napalm at the woman
       with the phone, which is up again, but without her
I wouldn't be thinking about consciousness, so I should be
       grateful, but there's a ping-pong game in my mind
between Ecstasy and Fury, which is pretty much the way
       in goes in my cranium—I loathe Jehovah, but I'm
out of my mind in love with the King James Bible, the "thees"
       and "thous" and the holy thought like a drop

in the sea of divine retribution, so blessed is the cell phone
        recorder on the second row, for she shall hear
Joshua Bell when she is boiling water for fusilli or sitting
        in the dentist's office waiting for a root canal,
or snuggling in her 200-count percales, and blessed
        are the synapses of the brain, that glorious highway
of molecules and nerve endings that constructs its castles
        of what happened and what might, and blessed
are Grieg and Wolfgang Mozart, who conjured their tiaras
        of notes and threw them in the air like the confetti
of a delirious nightingale, but fastened together by invisible
        threads that shimmer in the filaments of my ears,
the arpeggios, the triplets, the scales that sometimes fall
        from my eyes when contemplating the infinite
but usually stay plastered to my lids though I think I can see,
        but what is sight but an optical delusion of retinal
origin, and who can explain anything, though we try so hard
        to make sense of the falling pianos, black cats,
and the call of the owl in the night that sounds like a woman
        being strangled or the creak of the floor board
that could be warning of a thunderstorm about to break
        or a scythe in the hand of our darkest thoughts.

Ode on Being a Little Drunk at Parties

My brain is such a bully—wash your face, comb your hair,
       brush your teeth—but drink a glass of wine,
and my id rises up like Venus on the half shell, and says, "Baby,
       you're beautiful—even the stupid shit you say is smart,"
and this is when a party starts to shimmer, and if I'm lucky
       the music instructs me in the fundamentals of moving
through space and time, but with rhythm on this occasion,
       not the white girl cubist automaton beef jerky, oh, no,
arms akimbo, hips like silk kites in a summer sky, and I am talking
       to the gods—Aretha is unlinking my chains,
and Prince tells me what it's like to kiss, and if I'm extra lucky
       I'll find someone to buttonhole so I can talk about time travel,
because now I want to talk to the gods, as in—Athena,
       what's your problem, girl? You've got it all—
howitzer tits and a brain the size of Olympus—and all you do
       is cause trouble among the chuckleheads on earth.
Oh, I get it, it's hard to feel sorry for humans. We're a hot mess,
       and by the time some of us figure it out, we're playing
our endgames. But what's the story on Aphrodite? Is she stuck up,
       or what? And Hermes, I want those silver shoes
with the little wings—now that's a look, because with those shoes
       and a glass of champagne I could rule the world,
but who wants to be Zeus, with his beard, or Poseidon,
       riding the waves with his trident, not me that's for sure,
because I can barely make it through each cantankerous day
       with its roadblocks, red lights, and hurricane sirens—
god, the noise, so a party is like an invitation to take off
       your straitjacket, slip into a silver kimono,
and off we go to Monte Carlo, well, not there but the Biarritz
       of your dreams, which is like an opera by Donizetti

with lyrics by Cup Cake Delgado—a name I just made up
        out of the blue, which is one of my favorite activities,
maybe more fun than parties or wine or dancing to the songs
        that nail your scalp to the wall of your orangutan brain.

Ode to Juno, Queen of Heaven

Bad mood Mama, jagged goddess of steamed open letters, crabby
       czarina of the next move, how do I circumnavigate
this ragged world, because the roads are rippling with brigands
       and fools, nymphs and satyrs playing possum,
so where is the magic, my queen, where is the party, wine flowing
       and no one afraid of being turned into a snake? O shake
that rattle of rage because your man's strapping on his swan costume,
       his bull's horns, shimmering into a shower of gold. Don't blame
the girls. They were minding their own business when what happened?
       Danaë is still trying to figure it out, but Leda is riding it
like a wave. Go to hell, Zeus-meister, you stuffed sock of a god,
       no good to anyone but the hellraisers and yes-men
who clabber up the air on Mt. O. Oh, no, not another costume,
       and off he goes while you cook up a poison brew with toads
and red-capped mushrooms your nymphs have gathered from the forest
       floor, more than enough to send the whole human tribe
to Styx. So mix it up, baby, throw some psychedelic mojo
       in your vat of cherry Kool-Aid and tell us it's happy hour,
because we're waiting for an oblivion cocktail to help us pass
       on over to the other side, ride that wild monkey
into the delirious night, fight the pretty good fight against
       the puffed-up gods on their gerrymandered chariots
of gold. Hold the line! What's that? The Titans are back. We're
       in deep Shinola now, my queen. Lead us into temptation,
deliver us from our own worst impulses, like dressing up
       for the party of doom in the waiting room at the train station
before the next trip into a year of who knows what—war or peace,
       a new lease on the old body that still dreams of running wild.

Ode in Which Apollo Bitches about Caravaggio's *Medusa*

So you know it's him, right? That's pretty weird,
      to paint yourself as a woman with a hairdo
of snakes, and what about the shield, what's that say—
      I'm going to turn you into stone, and wait
if that doesn't work, I'll run you through with a sword?
      Being eternal, I have a few ideas about this dude
because I can watch his life like a movie—first,
      the still-lifes of fruit and flowers for the boudoirs
and drawing rooms of the rich Milanese, but how old
      does that get—being the contessa's lapdog,
so he escapes to Rome and falls in with the street people—
      the beautiful whore with the black hair
who became his Madonna, or the broken-down carrier
      who held up the cross and gambled with St. Matthew,
and those feet—didn't some cardinal turn down
      the Virgin of Loreto because the first thing you see
are the filthy feet of the pilgrims, and the first version
      of St. Matthew writing his gospel was bombed
in Berlin as I guess everything will be in the end,
      which reminds me that I've got to talk to Ares
about Putin, because that guy is out of control, but Ares
      thought Hitler and Mussolini were great, too,
not to mention Stalin, so it's not hard to see why
      the world's a mess, that and Aphrodite's mojo
working the center, because I have to say I preferred
      the world when there were fewer humans,
but that's me, canoodling with the muses is more what
      I have in mind—that Erato, man, when her fingers
start to skitter over the strings of the kithara, the songs
      just hop out like Easter bunnies in hula skirts

and when she and her sisters sing harmony, well,
      Beach Boys, move over, do-wop-a-doodle,
cha-cha-cha, but don't get me wrong, I love Caravaggio,
      the bad boy persona was a mask, but the rage
was real, the temper like a brush fire that's never really
      tamped down, ready to explode, because who
stabs someone because he's cheating at tennis, though it was
      more than that, but isn't it always, and Malta was good
for a while, that *Beheading of the Baptist*, with the sharp light
      of the executioner's torso, and the others, staring
at John, the blood spurting out of his neck, surrounded
      by the little people who do the dirty work of kings.

Ode to My Unquiet Mind in the Bowling Alley of My Soul

Chatterbox, pickpocket, Cracker Jack box
      with no prize inside, pink carnation
in the cup of the skull, karaoke night at the roller derby,
      all crash and Beatles covers—O mind, how I need
a seamstress to mend the couches in your bowling
      alley while I gutter over and over until I reach
the Underworld, and Persephone says, "Girlfriend,
      you need to try another sport, maybe archery
or speed walking," and I see how her mind is working,
      because I'd be planning my escape
from Danksville if I were her, too, but there's Spring,
      and Mommy's waiting with daffodils
and fresh bread, though Hades is a hunk, if kind of stinky,
      you know, like a pole cat died nearby
or he sat by a bonfire all night smoking spliffs
      while a Dylan wannabe droned on about death,
and there are lots of fires in hell, but house parties, too,
      popping up with homemade hooch that can knock
you into next Tuesday, where you, my mind, are waiting
      for me to straighten my skirt and put on
some lipstick and face the banshee, who is growing
      warts by the minute, and I think of Hamlet,
about whom someone says, "O what a noble mind
      is here o'erthrown," oh, right, it's Ophelia,
who had her own problems in this area, but don't we all,
      though some of us corral those wild horses better
than others, and maybe the banshee wants to be Wendy
      with her gaggle of lost boys or a Tri-Delt with Trey
and Kyle vying for her diacritical kink, but it's hard to know
      what anyone wants as we sit alone in front of the TV
of everything that's happened so far, looking for a new
      show, starring our beautiful hideous selves.

Ode to My Burning

You're a campfire on the outskirts of Hell, the gas burner
       on Satan's stove, the rigamarole of tinder and hate
bursting from TV screens. O sister, what fire rages
       in your furnace of tripe and gizzards, blood and ire?
You're in the choir of backseat drivers on the dirt road
       to a juke joint in the woods, hopped up on red-eye
whiskey and Coke, looking for trouble, and guess who's waiting
       for you in a cheap suit, doffing his creased-brimmed hat,
purring, "Hey, honey, wanna dance?" Oh, yeah, you're crisp
       as a deep-fried corn dog on the last day of the circus
when the high flyers come down from the trapeze,
       and the clowns take off their noses, bury them
in a dump by the radioactive lake, while you sleep with the lions,
       who have ditched their wigs to dream in caravans
of squalor and storm. Oh, baby, you're the raging neon
       on the strip in Vegas, lighting the low impact skies
with your sleaze and squeeze-box vino. You drop into a casino
       with its racket and roll of the dice, a shining slice
of the American bad-apple pie and bet everything on number three,
       because you're burning on your cross again like Apollo
for Daphne, his fingers touching her skin as it thickens and turns,
       but you're Daphne, too, as your arms become bark
and the dark pith of sap rises in your womb, and you see
       the earth for what it is—a river, a bell, a tomb.

Ode on the Wildest Word

No, sir, I am not your baby, not your twenty-dollar
      shot of tequila, not your excise tax on petroleum
jelly, your high-risk dirigible in the bomb-alicious
      sky filled with lies, the radio highs that last
three minutes tops, the shuck and jive of yes ma'am,
      doublethink spam, drink-the-Kool-Aid
Marxist sham, the wham up-against-the-wall
      cattle call of the true believers, left and right,
the slight lisp on the edge of doom. O no, Daddy-o,
      I cannot swim out to your island of swoon,
or the two-bit room in the Alligator Motel, that hell,
      with its sharp teeth and open jaws, the seesaw
back and forth between high noon and doom,
      that tune. No, baby, I'm sitting here all alone,
grown woman, looking back on all the tricks, the love
      sick delirium that blasts off to the moon
and then dissolves into a rule book and curdled milk,
      the silk cave of raven wings, the slinky
rinky-dink dance with death, the breathless sigh. O my,
      I'm saying no to the bye-bye lullaby,
half-hearted whisky-and-rye apocalypse afternoon,
      the harpoon-in-my-gut regret that says yes
to everything, sings soprano in the church choir, mucks
      in the mire outside the front door, the storm gutter
mutter of cant, the torn dress and sweaty hankering
      to do good, so here I am in a rococo imbroglio
of Hamlet and moonshine, the backwoods banter
      that begets shame, the no-name oblivion
of staying on the bus as it travels through the war zone
      and lets you off at what was once home.

Rage Ode

You know how it is when you're being so nice
        and the girl at the counter treats you like a slice
of cold pizza three days old with curled up pepperoni
        and a coating of mold, and you don't want to do it
but you're tired of her shit, so you turn on your heel
        and leave in a snit, blow down her cool
with your arctic squeeze, your Cleopatra frown, and your brain
        disease, but she doesn't care, cause she's sixteen,
her boobs sit high, and her mind's a screen of everything
        she'll never do, the screaming brats and the jerk who's
Mr. Libido in a dented wreck, waiting on the corner
        to cash her check. So what'd you expect
in your current state? Beautiful manners on a China plate?
        Get real, baby, that's not the scene, your Jane Austen
world's in smithereens, and Lady Murasaki's not at the door
        to usher you out to the ballroom floor, where Prince Andrei
waits in his tux his heart full of flowers, pants full of fucks.
        No, you're out of luck or you've had a stroke
because you're translating poems in a syncopated trope
        of Truth and Beauty or Beauty and Truth,
what's the difference when you're tightening the noose,
        and you blame Zeus and all those gods, Satan and Jehovah,
with their gym-ripped bods, Superman, too,
        though he knows how to shave, but what can you do
when you're born to crave a room of your own
        and plenty of time to lie in bed and make up rhymes,
but who should knock on your sanctuary door
        but the ghost of your mother and her Christian lore,
saying forget this world where a woman can rave,
        make up stories and ride the wave of her own palaver,

cause that's not real. You've gotta serve your god,
      serve your man, keep your house spic and span.
Oh, Mom, it can't be true, there's gotta be more
      than popping out babies and cooking up stews,
changing sheets and marking time, counting out your days
      in gin and limes. What about Italy? What about France,
going to parties to drink and dance? Juggling words like a circus clown,
      seven hundred verbs and a zillion nouns
spinning in the sky like an alien invasion, a shimmering mass,
      a mathematical equation or some crazy voodoo
in a smoking drink, shaken like a hurricane, ready to sink
      the whole human race in a pandemic rage, a virus blowing
through the human cage. Now's not the time to regret your life,
      slice it up with a kitchen knife. For the moment
we're all alive, though everything seems stupid and jive,
      and messed up, too, what with all the wars,
and the nasty talk by presidential boars. Let's glue
      the pieces together, my friends. I know that sounds
a little Zen with some Quaker do-wop on making amends,
      but who wants to be in a feudal state, a moat full
of plague and hearts full of hate. Let's save the elephants,
      and the bees, too, the gorilla, the cheetah, the whole
damn zoo, and the girl at the counter with her lethal cool.
      Oh, my sister, let's put down our weapons,
such as they are and make a truce before we go too far
      on this beautiful planet with its luminous star
because the night is storming and the coming age
      looms with darkness and armies of rage.

II.

Away! away! for I will fly to thee,
　　Not charioted by Bacchus and his pards,
But on the viewless wings of Poesy

-JOHN KEATS, "ODE TO A NIGHTINGALE" (SPRING 1819)

Make me thy lyre, even as the forest is:
What if my leaves are falling like its own!
The tumult of thy mighty harmonies

Will take from both a deep, autumnal tone,
Sweet though in sadness. Be thou, Spirit fierce,
My spirit! Be thou me, impetuous one!

-PERCY BYSSHE SHELLEY, "ODE TO THE WEST WIND" (OCTOBER 25, 1819)

Ode on *Paradis* and the Longing for a Place that Never Was

My sister and I are talking about our childhoods,
          which have the same cast of characters, but differ
so much that it's hard to believe we shared a bedroom
          for so long, and she often recounts how I threw up
on her, which I don't remember and neither did our mother,
          but my sister believes it so it's part of her story
but not mine, and I'm the only one who remembers our parents
          being in love or living in France in a little village in Alsace
called *Paradis*, and on our honeymoon, my husband and I
          drove through but I couldn't find the house, and twenty
years later, my mother and I made the same trip, and she
          couldn't remember where the house was either,
until she recalled a man who'd walk by every afternoon
          and urinate right across the street from our house,
which was kind of weird, but there was a lot of anti-American
          feeling, and when my mother remembered the guy peeing
that led us to the house, *toot sweet*, as she would say
          in years to come, along with *mangez*, the only French
she picked up, and our French landlords didn't want children
          in their fancy parlor but made one exception at Christmas,
and my mother created one of her magical holidays with a tree
          that dazzled, and my sister does remember how December
was a gorgeous time though she doesn't remember that one
          or the snow piled high, or how cold it was all year,
and when I think of that time, the Welsh word *hiraeth*
          comes to mind, or the longing for a place that never was,
and maybe that's what *Paradis* was, with fresh baguettes
          delivered every morning with milk and cheese,
and my mother so young and pretty, and there was a fireplace
          in the room next to the kitchen, where she fried chicken

and made pot roasts, and she would call us in from play
        with, *Mangez, kids*, which my sister remembers
from three years later in Virginia, De Gaulle having kicked us out
        of France because according to my mother America
wouldn't share the nuclear secrets with the French,
        and that's a big secret to share I'll grant you,
and France had just come through two wars which messed up
        the landscape, but time has healed those wounds,
and you see a lot of nuclear power plants, too, so someone
        let those secrets slip, and sometimes I wonder
if *Paradis* even existed, because my mother and father
        are both dead, and I'm the only one left
who remembers my mother slathering those baguettes
        with peanut butter no French child would ever eat,
and the little picnic place with merry-go-rounds in the water
        of the lake, and when my husband asked a man
who lived in *Paradis* about our landlord either Monsieur Iray
        or Siray, because my parents had forgotten, he said,
No Americans ever lived here, so now I'm thinking it was all
        a dream of paradise that my little girl's heart
made up out of nothing, even my young parents in love
        and the fire in the dark cave of their hearts.

Box Ode

Sarah is bartending at Waterworks, a local tiki bar,
      and tells us about the box a colleague has
with all the creepy notes men have slipped her,
      and I think most women have a box like this,

and if you're lucky it's not your body, and I think
      of what my own box might contain,
certainly the letter from the law professor's wife,
      the one she wrote when he asked me out,

and I said, "You're married," and he said, "We have
      an open marriage," and I thought, "Sure
you do," so I said I'd have lunch with him
      if his wife wrote me and said it was okay,

and I thought that would be the end of it, but he brought
      the note to the restaurant where I worked,
and I went out with him, but it was so boring that even
      he knew it was a stupid idea. How much

she must have wanted to get rid of him, and years later
      I met her again at a dinner party with a new
husband, and she didn't remember me, but I placed her
      around three in the morning, and my box

would have all the poems and drawings that men
      had tried to ply me with, though most of them
were pretty romantic, but what is romance but a trick
      on yourself, though a beautiful one,

and a lot of work to keep going but worth it when you're
        deep in the tunnels of your body
which lead to your heart box with all its swelling
        crescendos and arias of accordion classics

and your brain box full of Hamlet and refrigerator
        warranties and your cunt box with its bongo
drums and traffic sirens, and I love to think of Whitman's
        box of notes for "Song of Myself,"

all the little pieces floating like birds over the open sea
        of America before they were anything near
a typeset page or Pandora's box, which only became
        hers when she opened it to let loose the flies

of smallpox on an unsuspecting world, the locusts
        of polio, the invisible bubonic future
that has just knocked on our door, everyone's body a box
        of cells wanting to break free of its suit of skin.

Ode on Empty Lots and the Devils in the Bushes

O to have a mind like the empty lot by the True Fellowship
       Holiness Church that I pass on the way to work, filled
with grass and wild flowers, and bordered by Big Daddy's
       Barbecue and their party yard where the trucks
pull up every Friday—the corn-on-the-cob truck, the taco
       truck, and Mama Betty's fried chicken pickup—
and there's usually a band playing funk or blues, and sure
       there's a highway overpass on the other side,
a pork-barrel project that put another scar on the earth,
       but nothing's stopping the grass or the dandelions
or the Queen Anne's lace from dancing in the breeze
       from the exhaust and singing their little hallelujahs,
though there is the trash, wadded up receipts, and empty
       energy drinks thrown from passing cars,
and on Sundays the faithful begin their conversation
       with God, speaking in tongues, because who knows
what language the big guy speaks, not me for sure,
       though I'm partial to Athena and Aphrodite
or the Sumerian Inanna, who was the goddess of love
       and war, which are vying for a place in my mind
right now, and that empty lot is breaking out in brush fires
       that I have to stomp on like a pilgrim on a holy walk
around the great temple of Nanna at Ur or on the road
       to Compostela, the devil lurking in the bushes,
but where is he not lurking—on TV, the radio, the street
       corner—and his disguises still surprise me,
the poor little match girl with her mouthful of fangs
       or the chubby chanteuse who has the EQ
of a potted plant, but as Eudora Welty said, "It's a world,
       and we all live in it," so as the presidential candidates

board a new edition of The Ship of Fools, let's put our faith
in the birds, who sow the daisies and pink mallow
in their aimless flight over suburban lawns and empty
lots and gardens where the devils have no sway.

Ode on Drive-ins, the Pandemic, and Ovid in Exile

I want to sit in a car with a bag of popcorn and watch Antonioni
        kill his brunette in thirty minutes and then follow
his blonde through airless dead rooms in Sicily, to feel the nothing
        she feels, but in crumbier dives like Ovid on the boat
from Rome to Tomis on the Black Sea, writing to his friends to beg
        Augustus to cancel his exile, seasick, homesick, losing the city

he loved and hated, but what was his crime? *How can no one know?*
        I think as I pull my '55 Studebaker into its slot, hook up
the sound box, and watch a double feature of *Mulholland Drive*
        and *Celine and Julie Go Boating* with Mai Tais
from the tiki bar at the concession stand because this is the drive-in
        of my dreams, and I can have what I want,

and what is it about women on the big screen with a backdrop of sky—
        I'm talking to you, Greta Garbo, in *Ninotchka.* Marlene
Dietrich in *Witness for the Prosecution,* Barbara Stanwyck
        in *Ball of Fire*, but when Ovid lands, his new home
is not the center of the world—the forum, the Palatine,
        the Capitoline Hill—just a wooden fort on the edge

of the empire, barely holding back the barbarians, and at my dream
        drive-in I am watching *Barbarian Queen,* in which three women
free their people from Roman bondage, or maybe I'm watching
        Jules and Jim with Jeanne Moreau flaunting her bipolar beauty
through Paris and Germany. She's a free woman, but what is freedom?
        She's kind of bummed out and as miserable as Ovid is

when he reaches Tomis, which is now in Romania, but the big wigs
      are thrilled to have a famous poet come to stay,
so they put up with Ovid's sulking and after a couple of years,
      he discovers fishing, and even writes a book about it, now lost—
that's something I'd love to see, Ovid on fly casting,
      because he could spin a metaphor, and he's like Bill Murray

lost in a hotel in Tokyo or in Pennsylvania, waking up
      to the same day, until he has to change because he can't die
though he tries, and when Ovid wakes up, he isn't in Rome,
      but his head isn't on a stake at the forum either. *It was no crime,*
just a poem and an error—The Art of Love, and a slip at a party,
      the wine flowing and gossip raging, but you can't joke

about the emperor sleeping with his daughter, or his wife
      poisoning everyone between Augustus and her son Tiberius,
which are my pet theories about the "error," and then I read
      that Ovid wasn't exiled but made the whole thing up,
which is what I do every day, as in this drive-in with its Thunderbirds,
      Cadillac convertibles, and the cocktail bar with tiki torches,

but the last drive-in here closed years ago, and where is Louise Brooks
      when you need her? Where is the Dude, Duke, Rita, Gene
Hackman? Come back, Gene, you can do no wrong. I could watch
      The Conversation all night under the Milky Way,
pulsating with aliens . . . O fellow movie goers, let's open a drive-in
      and watch Bogart wipe the smile off Mary Astor's face,

The Wienie King give Claudette Colbert a wad of cash, so she can
        leave Joel McCrea and go to Palm Beach and find a rich husband,
and what about a double feature of *A Touch of Evil* and Cocteau's
        La Belle et la Bête? We could watch the flickering images
like Ovid writing to his readers when he realizes Augustus will never
        let him return to Rome—*I want to be with you any way I can.*

Ode on My Mother's Scissors

"Do you write?" asks the woman I'm sitting across from
        at Rivoire on the Piazza della Signoria, and I say,
"I do," so while everyone else at the table snorts and sputters,
        she goggles at me, trying to jibe what she's seeing
with what she's hearing, and I realize that what looks like
        a blonde from the Midwest is really the Buddha
with some information for me about the state of my what?
        —not soul, because that's not something he would talk
about, but maybe the one of the Six Perfections that gives me
        the most trouble—forbearance, which I finally figured
out meant patience, but it's probably just the First Noble Truth,
        which is the unsatisfactory nature of all things or *dukka*,
which always rears up when things seem to be going my way,
        or maybe she's not the Buddha at all but my mother
returned from the dead to puncture the circus-clown balloon
        of my ego, as she did when I handed her a copy
of a new book, and staring at me with her electric blue eyes,
        she said, "You know who wrote that," and I knew
she meant Jesus, which was easy for her to say, since she
        didn't have to cut and paste her consciousness
like a kidnapper fashioning a ransom note out of letters hacked
        from magazines, probably using her scissors that I keep
on my desk, which she used to cut out dresses for me
        and my sister and sew them on her little black Singer
sewing machine, which is also in my office, with its gold lettering,
        and I remember her sitting at the kitchen table stitching
doll clothes and curtains in the different places we lived all over
        the world, not to mention the costumes for Halloween
and plays, like the puffed sleeved empire dresses she made
        when I played Elizabeth Bennet or the Dutch Girl dress

I wore with the little wooden shoes for a pageant in the second grade,
      and even then those shoes were too small, but without
them the costume didn't work, but my mother packed my Keds
      in her big purse so I could run around with the other
kids when the curtain came down, and as I look at the woman
      across the table, how I wish she were my mother,
who had just shown up with her sewing machine, scissors, and Bible
      like a tinker from the other world so she could make me
the dress I've been looking for my whole life, like Flora's
      in Botticelli's *Primavera,* with all the flowers of spring unfolding
on diaphanous silk, or she could reach into her purse and hand me
      a pair of shoes that don't pinch or open her Bible
to Psalms 139:4—*Even before a word is on my tongue,*
      behold, Lord, you know it altogether.

Ode on Junk

When I landed at Wai'anae Elementary School, I learned
  that "junk" meant so much more than the metal
detritus of cars and trucks that were piled in junk yards,
  for one thing the game of Paper, Rock, Scissors
was called "Junk and a Po," and as you were swinging
  your fist, you'd sing, "Junk An'a Po, I Canna Show,"
which I didn't know came from the Japanese "Jan Ken Po,
  Ai Kono Sho," but there was so much I didn't know,
and I was avid to learn, as in "That pencil is junk" or "That
  movie is junk," which meant "no good" or "boring,"
and then there was the Chinese boat used to navigate rivers
  and carry cargo or boating parties, which appealed
to me, because drifting down a river on a boat with red sails
  would be an Alice in Wonderland dream, especially
with a picnic of cucumber sandwiches and tea and maybe
  a cherry tartlet for dessert, just to work in a Knave
of Hearts, and I sometimes think that my life's ambition
  might be organizing the perfect picnic,
with cold champagne and potato chips, my two current
  favorites, and just thinking about such an outing
starting out on a junk with magenta sails is enough to trigger
  the dopamine center of my brain, though "junk"
can also mean heroin, which is also a dopamine wizard
  but with much different results, and junk
can also refer to male genitalia, which I was thinking
  about while watching *Chernobyl* on television,
and after the meltdown, hunters were sent to shoot
  the radioactive pets and wild animals in villages
and farms in the contaminated zone, and the men fashioned
  lead coverings to protect their junk, though they'd

probably die of cancer before it even mattered, and the dogs
        would run up to them because they trusted humans,
which is really junk, as is a nuclear meltdown, though you
        might have to term that a mega-junk event,
and I often think that though I've never tried heroin,
        it might be perfect for the last month or so of life's
picnic, sailing down the river of forgetfulness, with cheese
        crackers, and maybe a glass of Sancerre, leaning
into the wind, as the azure sails of your little boat carry
        you into your last trip to that other world.

Ode to My Old Kitchens

for Stacey Harwood

O the meals I've made in you, some wretched,
      like the whole grain pasta that would have been great
wallpaper paste if a little lumpy, and some sublime,
      the divine seafood risotto with snapper, shrimp,
scallops, and oysters, and how hard it was to be a vegetarian
      until Italy with its grilled *melanzane*, caprese,
and fusilli with pesto, but by then I was eating meat
      again, mostly seafood, but there you were,
my kitchens, ready to help me learn how to be myself. How many
      English muffins have I toasted in you, slathering them
with butter and jam, first Smuckers strawberry or grape
      and then my homemade fig preserves or peach jam,
and how much coffee have I brewed, first drip and then machines
      until going to Italy I discovered the stovetop
espresso pot, and oh, my Italian kitchens, the one in La Tana
      with the stove I had to light with a match,
and the one on the *Via dei Mattinaia* that overlooked
      the courtyard of a hundred families, or the one
on the *via Santa Croce* with the vicious orange tomcat
      who waited till we left and then jumped in the window
and opened the door to the refrigerator and helped himself
      to the cheese, but back to America, to the little
house where I started my married life and discovered
      Marcella Hazan, making her pan-roasted chicken
and dancing with my new husband while the water
      boiled for the pasta, and in our next house
with the lime green Formica kitchen that we gutted
      and pulled up the linoleum to find pine subfloors,
you have been with me for so long, and in you I have baked
      and steamed and broiled and sautéed and sliced

have gone to India with her curries and raita and naan,
       hosted Georgian supras, with katchipuri
and wines redder than blood, and made baguettes,
       baked tarts sweet and savory, jammed
until I thought I'd go mad with the peaches and cherries,
       hardly remembering my kitchen on Park Street
where I taught myself to make pie crusts, cutting the butter
       into the flour with a kitchen knife, my window
overlooking Miss Eppes' house and her lovely flowers
       or Boulevard Street where I made soups—Deep
South Minestrone with okra and butterbeans, vegetarian chili,
       and split pea—though it helps to have a husband
who loves to eat, and I just found the recipe for bran muffins
       tucked into an old book—how many tins
of those did I bake, stuffed with raisins, or the buttermilk
       cake I just baked with blueberries, and the popcorn
I've popped, and the spices I've collected, and the cookbooks
       that are spilling onto the floor because the bookcase
is full, as I am after dinner and sitting out in the garden
       of Eden that opens out of my back door
and the 300-year-old oak tree dripping with Spanish moss,
       the mockingbird of my mind that's sitting on a branch,
chattering about how buzz-saw crazy the world is as we sit
       at the table and cut into a deep-dish blackberry pie.

Ode on My Half Sister

I'm in my front yard admiring the hundred ruffled
      red-and-white parrot tulips I planted in December
when my sister pulls her car under the two magnolias
      near the road and runs up and says she has just talked
to a woman who we thought was a first cousin,
      but "Guess what? The DNA says she's our half-sister,"
and after a little mental scrambling we figure that our father,
      years before he met our mother, had sex
with his older brother's wife, who I remember from photos
      as looking a lot like our mother, and there he was,
eighteen, handsome as Tarzan with his swimmer's body,
      ready to ship off to war in the Pacific, and she,
a minister's wife without children, her husband off tending
      to his first church, and she sitting in the back yard
with our father, who could always pull in women
      with his sad story, wide shoulders, and slim hips,
but this is the first time, and she feels her eyes brimming
      with the voice of the boy abandoned by his mother
when his father died, and her own husband was fifteen,
      almost a man, but this boy was five, and he'll
be dead soon in the war, so they go back to the bed
      he's been sleeping in and afterwards they swear
they'll tell no one, and they don't, and the next year
      she has a daughter, but he isn't killed in the war
and returns and marries another woman, and there they are
      in a photograph, three brothers and their wives,
a sister, and the oldest brother's little girl, a beanpole,
      eight years old, and no one knows, not the mother
or my father or my mother, but now we know everything,
      but maybe we don't, because there are so many

stories within every story, like the archway in Istanbul
        that was being repaired, and the workmen found
a piece of parchment sealed inside an earthenware flask
        and when it was opened and translated
from the ancient script, it was found to be instructions
        from the great architect Sinan, who 400 years
before had estimated when the arch would crumble
        and so wrote to the architects of the future
to describe how he had balanced the stones and cut
        them and even the location of the quarry,
and this letter is like finding a note from Shakespeare
        saying they had these redheaded twins
in their company, one an idiot and the other who could melt
        butter with his voice, and only in that moment
would Viola and Sebastian be believable on the stage,
        but when I look at my DNA report, our half-sister
has the about the same percentages as our other first cousins,
        but my real sister doesn't want to believe me
because it isn't as good a story, but for a moment
        it was true, and the mysteries that hide
in the closed archways of our bodies were broken open
        and revealed a love story in what seemed to be
an ordinary photograph of three brothers and a sister
        who had put their lives together after a war
that had torn the world apart and put other families
        in mass graves that are still being discovered
in the flask of the earth from which we, like fools, expect
        spring to erupt even after the coming plague.

Ode to My Brother Who I Haven't Spoken to in Thirteen Years

My brother who everyone says is so charming,
        which is true, until he isn't, and then he becomes
a black bird in the dark night on the slopes
        of a live volcano that is rumbling and filling
the room with the sulfur of his untamed mind.

My brother who lost twenty years the way I lose my keys.

My brother who lived in Paris with a violinist who kicked
        him out of the apartment for five hours every day
while she practiced so she could play bluegrass in Tex-Mex
        restos that were dotting the city like jalapenos.

My brother who loves Peugeots and has bought seven
        I know about and is restoring one now in Chicago
where he moved after he left Paris.

My brother with the broken violin of his heart,
        with the five-alarm fire in his brain, who painted
a portrait of our mother wearing our father's glasses
        that she filled with her prescription after he died.

My brother with the crooked fingers, with his buzz-saw
        tongue, with his hair like Rasputin, with his French-
aristocrat goatee, with his penchant for decapitation.

O guillotine in the center of every room. O shipwreck
        off the coast of Patagonia. O Papillion
on Devil's Island with the rats and mosquitoes.

Where is the baby I held in the black-and-white photograph
        in New Orleans? Where is the boy who went with me
to see Jimi Hendrix play *The Star-Spangled Banner* on his knees
        backwards over his head and die the next year in London?
Where is the boy on the top bunk in Honolulu, listening
        to the radio as if it were playing a message from God?

Ode to the Radio

Anarchy incarnate, are you sending out signals
      from Alpha Centauri or from the dumpster
      behind the Sugar Shack with its banana skins,
      forgotten fries, and balled up greasy wrappers?
Bop king of the divided night, *wherefore art thou*
      dark prince of the blues? Oh, right there, hanging out
      smoking cigarettes in cars, rolling out the zeitgeist
      of late sixties cool on the waves of teenage angst.
Carnivorous crabdaddy of the cantankerous street, every car
      has your little engine of annihilation on its dashboard,
      cranking out doo-wop on top of disco, country twang
      canoodling with bosa nova, rattling out
Delirious arias, as when the Queen of the Night rises up
      like a Valkyrie and out-shouts every Brunhilde
      on the planet. Oh, baby, you've been there,
      felt its rhythms on your cranial drum, taken
Elocution lessons from Sinatra, notes on sorrow from Joni
      Mitchell, because all you really want to do is live
      from moment to moment on the river of song,
      the stake-through-your-heart blues vernacular,
      or, let's face it, the carnivalesque fun-house
Freak-out on the dance floor that not only shakes
      your booty but flips your switch, makes you swoon
      as the harpoon pierces your lungs, that vampire
      moment you've been waiting for your whole life,
      when you are nobody at last,
Going nowhere on the vast ocean of C minor. O Mozart,
      you've got me on my knees in the dungeon
      with all the Time Lords' dark thoughts,

Hades' hacked shades, his remoulade of prayer and lust,
> that busker whose god you've lost and found,
> ground into the dust of every word you've read,
> the Dead Sea Scroll of your body's cave or your arctic
Ice queen heart that doesn't even begin to care, stares
> into the blasted eyes of your mother and all the women
> who've pumped on the brakes at Stop signs, followed
> the rules, put new spark plugs in their decrepit
Jalopies only to learn that rust never sleeps, keeps spinning
> out its dead red crust no matter how hard you scrub,
> while the lazy sluts dream of their most dismal
Kinks, and scheme of doing nothing but floating
> through the day, reading Russian novels all night,
> Lady Day crooning on her island of lost
Love so it's autumn in New York no matter where you are,
> and though you ask, "How free am I anyway?"
> you still run after it, like a groupie after a guitar god
> because no matter how lost you are
Music is a ladder that will help you climb from the darkest
> cavern, and when the spondulicks run out or love,
> there's someone out there who explains you to yourself,
> the eternal winter that's spreading through the land and every
"No!" out of the mouth of doom, because as the Buddha says,
> you can't get no satisfaction, and though you try to tamp down
> the oompah band in your heart, it just keeps on beating
> its worn-out bongo drums like Bozo the Clown
On amphetamines, and now someone is singing, "Get Down,"
> and could that possibly be James Brown,
> Mr. Super Bad, Mr. I'm-So-Bad-I'm-Good,
> Mr. Let's-Wreck-the-Whole-Damn-Planet

Playing now on the chaos station, that is W-MESS,
       where you dream of being the only white girl
       in the back-up singers behind Leonard Cohen in London,
       because when you sing in the shower, you are right there
       in the spotlight, with Kiri Te Kanawa, Tina Turner, and
Queen, belting out the arias that are the soundtrack
       of all our heartbreaks and lousy choices, the lazy ones, too,
       that turn on you like a broken theme-park ride and all
       you can do is scream into the toxic night
Return to sender or *Why don't we do it in the road*,
       and you *are* the radio, sending your song
       into the wrung-out world, and it's hard to tell
       when all your love's in vain, or that pagan dream girl
Sappho would have never had to beg Aphrodite for a leg up
       or Horace ask the same goddess to flick Chloe
       on her hoity-toity ass, and I'm telling you there's a voice,
       coming out of a little box in my heart, that is translating
       Beethoven into bebop, Schubert into Coltrane, so spin your
Turntable into the terrible night, with bombs flashing over Kyiv,
       buildings crumbling in Turkey, children screaming in Gaza,
       because we are all drowning in a sea of misinformation,
Underwater and out of air, or maybe we are walking out
       to St. Audrey's fair with all the cheap tawdry trash
       that flows through our lives like a river of noise,
       and was it Jesus or maybe Dylan who said,
Verily, I say unto you, the servant is not greater than his lord,
       but who is the servant and who is the lord, because I've
       been the scullery maid and the queen, and both have
       their pluses, though the serving wench can slip out
       of the castle and dance the night away

While Her Majesty has to stay home and polish her diamonds,
        maybe waltz around the ballroom with the German
        ambassador, an ally now, but who knows tomorrow
        when the footservant brings in the mail, and she screams,
"Existentialist telegrams be damned, I'm going to the beach,"
        and there she is swimming out to sea, gray clouds
        banking on the horizon, as far as you can see, because
You and everyone else have figured out the end is coming,
        so do you swim out to meet it or build a fortress
        to keep it at bay or pray to one of those errant
        numbskull gods—Apollo, Athena, you know,
Zeus and his motley crew—and what's playing
        on the radio as they pull you up to Mt. Olympus
        by your hair, screaming *There must be some way*
        out of here, because there is and there isn't,
        but whatever you do, don't look back.

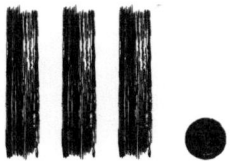

III.

The god of wine is at this party, and, if we're lucky,
  the goddess of love will turn up, too, and when
the lamps are lit, the Graces will dance until the sun
  puts out the dazzling stars one by one.

-HORACE, ODE 3.21 (23 BCE)

We shall see the grave of love as a lovely sight
and temporary near the elm that spells the lovers' names
in roots and there'll be no more music but the ears in lips
and no more wit but tongues in ears and no more drums
  but ears to thighs

-FRANK O'HARA, "ODE TO JOY" (1957)

No decree or creed can outlaw you
As you take every living thing apart. Little
Master of earth, no one gets to heaven
Without going through you first.

-YUSEF KOMUNYAKAA, "ODE TO THE MAGGOT" (2000)

Ode for the End of the Party

What happened to the music—the pop, bebop, twang
      of Django, fangs of women laughing, two men
banging heads in the street, throwing up on the red Mustang,
      and then the champagne you found in the back
of the refrigerator that I drank from the cup of your mouth?

O party, where did you go, the acid dropped in a million molecules
      of searching for the theory of everything only to see
Aristotle across a crowded room. Where are you Sin,
      you sailor in the back of the boat, ship of cool, shipwreck,
shipshape in the morning with its hot buzz of flyspecked nothing?

Where are my eyes that could read in the dark? My feet that could walk
      into the deepest cave and come out with all the animal voices
alive on my tongue: tiger tantrums, lion sneers, macaw squawks
      searing the sky with their stories of strangled blood?

I'll tell you this, there was a party once that spanned the globe—
      the Luna moths were out, and constellations
descended to earth, phosphorescent creatures swimming in the ocean,
      covering my body like a ballgown of light. There were birds
drinking green from the sky, brushing dirt from my eyes,

but now the days are ripe with contagion, our moats drawn,
      chickens growing wings to fly, little cats twitching in their nests,
dreaming of wild nights in the moonlight shimmering with fog,

because once we were golden, our lips red with the juice of God,
      our ears filled with the hymns of creation, but now our bodies
are dry as the desert, waiting for the vultures of time, translating
      Zulu into Hebrew, Thai into High German gobbledygook,

but once there were oaks from Canterbury to London, great aching trees;
  once there were so many birds that the skies of the new world
were black at noon with their flight, once prairie grass covered the belly
  of the land, but *now we are engaged in a great civil war,*
all parties wrestling in a theater of mud, while our assassin struts
  the stage. *Tis now the very witching time of night.*

O Bacchus—Loudmouth Lord of the Middle of the Party,
  Killer of Bummed-Out Stinky Thinking, Son of the Zig-zag
Electric Hoochie Coo, King of the Purple Sky over Milwaukee—
  I need some *vino experimento* in my veins, I need some
Shake-It-Up, Baby, a little night music, a close encounter
  with the dark prince in the dark center of my heart,

because he is siphoning the juice from my oranges, the wine
  from my sacrament, the pong from my *pinga*, the pretty
pieces of the puzzle I could never finish. O party, I thought
  you'd never end. I thought I'd walk to Valhalla

on my own two feet, but here I am on a rocking boat, tossed
  in a cyclone between my ears. Farewell, my lovely fiesta
of red drinks and endless talk about delirious nothing, I was your
  number one girl for a moment. I was your queen.

Ode in which Athena Tells Off Aphrodite at the Steak and Shake on Jackson Bluff Road

What is it with you, 'Phro? You ask me out to talk
        about Apollo, and the first guy you see,
poof—I'm nothing. I should have known when I saw
        that outfit. Gold lame for a chocolate shake,
fries, and then a movie at the mall? And the guy—his lines
        were moronic. "Are you movie stars?" We're frigging
goddesses. We have an inner light, plus we're both seven
        feet tall—well, I am. You're probably six-five,
but still. You know, he reminds me of that shrimp Paris,
        scraggly beard and eyes like a pool at the Econolodge
on the truck route. Men are nothing but trouble. I should
        know. My dad is a headache, and only Ares
can stand up to me, but he smells like all the dead
        in the wars he's started since the beginning
of time. You've probably spent a thousand nights
        with him. If your husband catches you, you'll be
dust, but it must be nice to just kitten through the world,
        snuggling up to tomcats and lions and looking
in the mirror. Oh, I know, I'm beautiful, too, but scary
        like a tiger or a lioness, pacing the savannah
looking like I want to tear the throat out of some hyena
        or wildebeest, and then eat it raw in the afternoon
sun while my kittens tumble in the dust—O yeah, that's me,
        and I can't hide it no matter how much makeup I wear.

Ode on Conversation

O how I love to talk to someone whose mind is a swift boat
      on the rushing tumult of the moment, dipping my hand
into the water of another's river, diving into their stream
      as they dive into mine, and the best are like a tagine,
with maybe the meat of poetry, the spices of gossip, the salt
      of family stories, and the carrots and potatoes of politics,

and a few surprises like the cinnamon that you can taste
      for a few seconds and then moves on as you jump
from the present scandal to the recipe for pizza dough
      to why Shakespeare didn't call *Julius Caesar*
Brutus since he's the main character or Omar in *The Wire*
      saying about Ares and Mars, "same dude, different

name," because the caverns of the mind go deep, the present
      consorting with all the gods of the past as when
in a taxi in Florence "Layla" comes on, and I ask the driver
      to crank it up, and he says, "Questa musica non finirà mai,"
which means this music will never end, though I would have
      said, "die," but what is death but a change in topic

in an already rushing tumult, and love always ends,
      as it did for Eric Clapton and Pattie Boyd,
or as Mycroft Holmes says to Sherlock, "All lives end.
      All hearts are broken. Caring is not an advantage,"
and yet we do care, but why, and "why" seems to be
      the word that rises like an orca off the coast

of Iberia capsizing sailboats, and why wouldn't they
        since the waters have been theirs since the ancients
began to venture into the deep, and I remember seeing
        Albert King at a concert at the old Wrestling Arena
in Honolulu, and he was on a bill with the Paul Butterfield Blues
        Band with Elvin Bishop and Michael Bloomfield though

I hardly knew what the blues were then, but that conversation
        was jumpstarted when King began to play "Born
under a Bad Sign," because who wasn't, especially Duane
        Allman, who a year after he translated King's guitar
on "As the Years Go Passing By" into the initial chords
        of "Layla," died on his motorcycle, and aren't we

all looking for signs, like the Etruscans translating
        the flight of birds into omens, or when Calpurnia saw
Caesar's death in a dream, which didn't stop the blood
        from flowing, and did you know that Brutus
may have been Caesar's son by the beautiful Servilla,
        which throws a spanner in the works, a phrase

I probably picked up from the English mystery novels
        I'd read to cool my brain after something
gnarly like *The Possessed,* which is a better title than
        The Devils, but my Russian is almost nonexistent,
though I could ask my friends Marina and Olga to weigh in,
        and wouldn't that be a conversation to have,

and then there's the Bengali word "adda," free-floating talk
      that can last for hours but with tea and snacks,
  though I'd prefer a cocktail called *Off with Her Head*, a heady mix
      of gin, Crème de Violette, and lime juice, but sometimes
I feel like Caesar when he said, "Et tu, Brute," because betrayal
      is in the air, but maybe he was remembering

the moment as a young man when Brutus was conceived,
      and in that moment of pleasure, he was putting in motion
 his own death, a moment the French call *la petite mort,*
      and they are entirely correct, as are the Italians
with their *dolce far niente,* though who would want to do nothing
      all the time, for then the sweetness would turn to boredom,

and God knows what mayhem might ensue, spearheaded by Ares
      who disguised as Mars is at loose on the world,
and if only Aphrodite could sweettalk him into substituting
      the little death for the big one, we could all stop talking
and head home through the steaming streets of Kolkata
      caring about everything and nothing in the same breath.

Want Ode

I want to walk into a drug store and buy all the bumblebees
        made between 1960 and now because I'm not feeling perky
today or any day, my body like an eighteen-wheeler that hauls
        orange juice from Florida to Milwaukee in January,
skidding into Toyotas and Kias, flattening them like the flies
        that circle my head and drink from the cup of my eyes,

but I want to be those flies buzzing like a fire alarm at 3am,
        my brain blazing and my body following like a hungry dog,
walking through a city where I don't speak the language,
        every word a slap in the face or an invitation to a party
in a deserted mansion where the dictator beheads the poet,
        and his wife stabs him in his bath, eats blood oranges

and weeps. I want to swim across the Bosphorus with Byron,
        to be his club foot and the ink in his pen as he writes
Don Juan, I want to be the craggy Armenian verbs
        he is breaking his mind against on the island
of San Lazaro in Venice, the mornings of fog over the lagoon.
        I want to be the bread he tears with his teeth,

the fever raging through his veins at Missolonghi,
        because there is only luck to explain why I am
still here and not in some kind of jail with a dark-haired
        daughter who loathes me even more than I loathe
myself. I am roaming the outer edges of my own mind,
        and I want to bury my thoughts in the dark corridors

of my dreams, break through the ghosts of my dead,
　　　like sheets on the line outside our house
when I was ten. I want to be a cat with a tail that curls
　　　around my feet, who goes out wilding every night
with an orange tom, a scar across his nose, who takes me
　　　to the juke joints with deep dirty blues and drinks

so rough I wake up with my voice two octaves lower
　　　than when I went to bed with Etta James in my throat.
I want to step into Beethoven's filthy apartment with the pizza
　　　boxes stacked on the floor and listen to him pound
his piano into splinters. I want to be the splinters and the pain
　　　in his gut that becomes the opening of his Fifth.

I want to be the immortal beloved, to smell your body
　　　when I first knew you wanted me, that same yeasty pong
that drove me mad with desire, because I want to stop time,
　　　start time, make time, pass time, want to blow my past
to smithereens and still remember everything in Technicolor detail,
　　　so I'm asking when will this wanting stop, why is it like

the stars above as we walk along the Tevere, Rome stretched out
　　　in all her dark glory, while we talk about Caravaggio
and Keats, the razzamatazz which gathers luster in the vast fields
　　　of sleep. I want to dream and never wake, run and never stop,
spin my top along the edge of swoon, walk with the street corner gods,
　　　singing their sideshow songs that fuel the endless night.

Ode on the Rilke Metro Stop in the Paris of My Dreams

In this dream we're in Paris, driving around in a car,
       which is a nightmare, so we ditch the Citroën
and take off on foot, though this is not the Paris we know so well
       but a fifties futuristic idea of the city with flying cars
or are they mechanical birds—it's hard to tell, and we arrive
       at the metro station, which looks like an Art Nouveau

space shuttle, a mash-up of *The Jetsons* and *The Time Machine*,
       and I look up to try to figure out where we are,
and the metro sign says Rilke, and I know this is a dream,
       whose message is what—you must change your life?—
which is pretty much always true, and I think, what's next,
       a Kafka metro stop where we step out in to a Prague

of dapper insects, or the Keats Metro stop that's moonlit
       and trembling with nightingales, or the Brontë Metro Stop,
that opens on the moors, and look, there's Sylvia Plath
       and Ted Hughes wandering around in their different dreams
of love, not to mention dreams of the future, because medieval dream
       scholars divided dreams into two categories—one a Rolodex

of your day with its jumble and flight, and the other a mystery train
       of oracles and visions—and that's the one I'm riding now
through the suburbs of my mind, looking out on the high rises
       of 1974, 1988, and 2004, and wasn't that when we lived
in London, so I get out and take an elevator to the twenty-third floor
       and step on to the stage of a play of my midsummer

night's dream and being lost in Venice that night of the big storm,
        rain driving its power into the ground of my consciousness,
the water rising over the bridges, and if I drown, will I find myself
        on the train again in a plush seat across from the smiling face
that will pull off her mask and reveal the cicatrice of her akull,
        and I have two choices—scream or close my eyes

and hope she's gone when I open them, and poof, in her place
        is my mother, and I say, "Mom, what was that all about?"
 and she opens her mouth to let fly the ravens of retribution,
        but in their beaks are messages from all the poets I love,
and Horace tells me to open a bottle of wine and lie back
        and look at the sky through the trees, while Neruda

cuts open a tomato for the salad, and Emily takes a cake
        out of the oven, and we sit down at a long table
in the country on an afternoon in May with Chekhov and Ovid,
        who has caught the fish in the waters near Tomis,
and Tolstoy who has a plate of mushrooms, everyone alive, even Sylvia

who sets down a roast and potatoes and her famous lemon pie,
        and we toast the past because that train has left the station,
and all we can do is keep riding this one until it is either blown up
        by brigands or pulls into the town at the end of the line,
and there's my mother and Rilke, too, and he says, "Do you
        know each other?" And she says, "I know everyone."

Ode to the Last Kiss in Venice

I dream my parents have a restaurant in a city
       that is a mashup of Honolulu, where they lived,
and Venice, which they never even visited, and their bistro
       is on a very Italian piazza or I guess I should say
campo because we're in Venice or a dream Venice,
       which you could say about the real city,
especially when summer ends, and I know what this dream
       means because a few weeks before we were
riding home from dinner, and the other couple are talking
       about their fathers, and they ask me, "What about
your dad?" and I say, "He was a loser," and right away
       I want to bite off my tongue, because in the eyes
of the world he didn't do much, but he was the sweetest man,
       loved poetry, bought the book that changed my life,
took me to the beach, taught me to swim, treated others
       with kindness, was elegant, and looked good
in a suit, which is how he lured my mother, who loved him
       until the end though he exasperated her
with his fecklessness, and if she had been sitting beside me
       in that car, she would have said, *I taught you*
better than that, and she did, but I often fail to heed her
       voice in my head, trust someone who is trolling
for a soft spot where they can stick in a knife, but love
       can lead you astray, and in that dream restaurant
in Venice, my mother looks up from the books, and says,
       "We got a great deal, because the former owners
lost their liquor license, and since we don't drink, we don't
       serve alcohol," and I look around at the miserable
diners, with their glasses of tap water and sodas, and think
       I'd never eat here, but I did for the first eighteen

years of my life, and ate well, never missed what I didn't
      know, and my dad is the host at the restaurant,
looking sharp in an Italian blazer and an ascot, and he
      turns to me with such a look of love on his face
and kisses me good-bye as I step into the gondola of sleep
      which ferries me to my bed in the present moment,
that kiss still warm on my cheek like a greeting
      from a land to which I, too, will be traveling soon.

Ode to Words for the Body

Having just read an article that called for changing
       the names of the human female orifices
to *front hole* and *back hole*, I have stopped to ponder
       language, and though *vagina* and *anus*
are not two of my favorite words, I'm not ready to say,
       "Double-plus good" to this linguistic foray,
and I'm thinking about Ludwig Wittgenstein, whose ideas
       about language began in the *front hole/back hole,*
just-the-facts-ma'am school but later saw language as play,
       though he did say, "I don't know why we are here,
but I'm pretty sure that it is not in order to enjoy ourselves,"
       which I can't agree with at all, because why are there
beauty and play if not to have fun, so here's to the body—
       which is a party animal par excellence, yes, you,
mouth—my pucker lapper, rosy red woodpecker
       of nerve endings and laughter, my ha-ha factory,
double dirigible of lips, tongue cave, tooth booth,
       talking machine, and you, eyes—lying cameras
of the brain's deluded mirror, flutter cups of unutterable
       nothings, and ears—wax catchers, amaryllis of Mozart
and bebop, Vertigo palace, radio fact checker of the coming
       apocalypse, and nose—sniffer out of fresh bread
and autumn's crisp mornings, not to mention breasts—
       Valkyries, va-va-voom vortex of velvet croissant,
and you, vagina—sex orchid, unfolding hibiscus,
       vulva *incroyable,* leading to the thighs—Minoan columns
of the body's lions gate, and knees—knobby outposts
       on the pathway to the feet, sometimes on the earth,
which many call dirt and others *terra firma*, which we first see
       when we descend from the front hole, sliding slick
into this land of a thousand dances—our skin canoe carrying us
       into the scream of our first morning on earth.

Ode to the Lost House

Why do I leave you deep in sleep and move to another house,
        one that has a roof with holes, a live-in possum family,
a kitchen with a floor of snapping teeth, and a secret door
        to the underworld that looked like a pantry
when the realtor showed us through, but now I dream of you,
        my former house, where I cooked so many meals,
danced to all my 45s, lay under the giant oak with Patsy
        and purred into the evening, but in another dream
I drive by you, and you look so small and disheveled,
        your yard shaggy, and I don't remember that trailer
next door, or the dogs roaming in packs, and ghosts
        smoldering in windows like transparent film noir
extras waiting for their cue to strangle me in the bathtub,
        so, thank God I don't live there any more,
but my new house has soulless lime green linoleum
        on every floor and running up walls, ready for bleach
after the stab fest that I've been dreading for the last fifty years,
        and the man with the knife, I know him—Jesus,
who would have thought he would look so much like my father,
        who was so kind in real life, and why can't I wake up,
because now I'm in a car looking for the houses I barely remember,
        talking to Wayne in Algiers, who lives in the place
my mother and father rented when I was born in New Orleans,
        or driving in France and stopping at the village to find
the house we lived in when I was five, or the little pink house
        on Puhano Street in Wai'anae when the plumerias
were blooming. O my lost houses, the little apartments
        that were torn down to make lawyers' offices,
the gardens plowed and covered in asphalt, how can I be sure
        that you were ever there or that these walls
won't crumble to nothing during the night in the hurricane
        of thoughts ricocheting around my head.

Ode to English, Amok and Running

Anglo Saxon, you rampaging Viking hunk with blue eyes,
      muchos gracias for your 500 words we use every day—boy
and girl, cow and pancake, all the curse words, and skunk,
      monk, lunk, funk, because English, you had some funky
beginnings—while the rest of the world was using alphabets
      you had runes, and your first sentence wasn't written
until 450 AD on a coin—*This she-wolf is a reward to my kinsman,*
      which means what? The coin, a dog, or a sharp-
tongued woman? Who knows, English, but you grew fast,
      put on weight, opened for business, and set up your

Bully pulpit of mercantile lingo—derivatives, assets, revenues,
      liens, debt consolidation, cash flow, collateral,
break-even point, only no one does, just big daddy Mr. Moneybags,
      Scrooge McDuck, the Bezos-a-rama, ka-ching, that forgets
the little languages that fed into the mighty Mississippi, like

Celtic, a banshee screaming in the bog, the clabbered milk,
      hooligan smashing the night to smithereens, after hours
in the pub drinking whiskey, the water of life, a party galore.

Damn your warmongering rants, the *sieg heil* salute to jackboots,
      all the AK-47 dirigible shit storms in countries too forlorn
to have an exit visa to another place, the drone empires of potentates,
      dictators, oligarchs, Visigoths, demon kings, hopped-up
engineers of the out-of-control-200 mph-train of the coming

Eco-apocalypse, which is already here, etching out its onslaught
          of fire—Rattlesnake, Scorpion, Slink, El Dorado,
Fox, Mojave, Zaca, Caldor—and the deluges—Ida, Eta, Bertha,
          Michael, Cristobal, Fred, Delta—the hurricane and virus,
ramping through our blood streams, like Zeus throwing a tantrum
          on Mount Olympus, Poseidon and Ares his wingmen.

French, you, invaded in 1066, tried to obliterate the native speakers,
          but Anglo-Saxon showed you when you married
its beautiful blondes and forgot the Paris that had already forgotten you
          though you live on in our legal gobbledygook and in the words
we use to pick apart the world in our brains—philosophy, ontology,
          oncology, hermeneutics, physics, phenomenology. Jesus!

Get this, English, you are like the winner of the pie-eating contest
          at the county fair, you don't care how you look as you
gobble up the apple, pumpkin, blueberry, blackberry, cherry pies,
          because you're a mess and proud of it, strutting your
dumb-ass diatribes all over cybersphere, making cracked-brained
          connections, in love with the marginal, insane

Hullabaloo of a world gone amok, from a Malay word, *amuk*,
          meaning frenzied attack, as when mobs go out on
the streets and kill as many people as they can, so school shootings
          and supermarket rampages have a history as do words like

Icebox, which just happens to be more fabulous than
         refrigerator, and my mother never made the switch,
so I still use it when I'm talking to my husband about dinner,
         a linguistic toast to my mother, who used to say,
That's the oldest story in the book, and I'd ask, *What book?*
         What story? And she would roll her eyes and let me

Jabber on, stringing words together like a double lei of lingo
         zinging with Hawaiian pidgin, which is a ratatouille
of English, Hawaiian, Chinese, Japanese, and a couple of other
         languages, so when a TV announcer says, *The governor*
covered his okole on that one, you know he's saying, *He covered*
         his ass, and my favorite Hawaiian word is *kuleana,*
which means responsibility, so when someone tries to bully
         you into doing something you don't want to do, you
can say, *Hey, man, that's not my kuleana*, which sounds
         so James Dean with a little aloha thrown in. Oh, English,

Kleptomaniac lingo thief, bring your pajamas to the slumber
         party of all the words you have pillaged or stolen,
all the linguistic loot (Hindi), and as you light your cigar, you are
         lighting the Spanish *cigaro*, which they stole from
the Mayan *sicar*, and what about cookie (Dutch), wanderlust,
         (German), lemon (Arabic), ketchup (Chinese),
penguin (Welsh), karaoke (Japanese), but while you're at it
         why not steal the Swedish *mangata,* the trail moonlight
makes on water, or *Schadenfreude*, oops that's almost English
         now, or will be in twenty years, and don't get me started on

Latin, Lord of All the Stuck-up language we use to mean
          nothing, and I know you went through the mill of French
to land on English shores, but I hate your *acumen*, why not say
          common sense, or drunk instead of *bibulous*,
using words the impecunious don't understand so you can
          bamboozle them with your erudition—you are ubiquitous,
pickpocketing the hoi polloi in their shacks and bungalows
          while you hobnob with the gods. Oh, English, you're

Messed up for sure, but it's a hot mess like that boy
          on the corner with the slick hair and slim hips. Forget
what he'll look like in ten years, all that Bud going right to his gut,
          because he's sexy now, his sneer so cool, his libido hot,
and so are you, English—I love how chaotic you are,
          how you can throw a chain saw, a flaming tiki torch,
an accordion, and a monkey wrench up in the air and juggle
          them while a mariachi band plays Beatles covers in the

Night of our party-hearty apocalyptic end game Armageddon,
          because we're having fun, but it's a kind of fireworks-
going-off-in-your-hands-after-drinking-too-many-margaritas-
          and-ending-up-behind-the-Taco-Bell-by-the-dumpster
fun, which seems like a beatnik paradise until the Pharisees show
          up screaming for your crucifixion. Oh, English, I love your

One-note onomatopoetic honk, beep, vroom, clang, boom,
          bang, zoom of motorcycle gangs gone haywire,
riding the flat roads of the American West, tattoos ablaze
          in the setting sun, John Ford on amphetamines, so

Put it here, pard, let's review what we've learned so far—pretty
        much nothing, but we're still surfing the lingo sea,
waiting for the big waves to roll in from the Pacific and building
        a fire on the beach of our own stupidity. Here's a pop

Quiz for all you cognoscenti—Why is English so elephant-
        in-the-room ginormous? a) English cannot stop snacking,
b) English is a slut who will have sex with anyone, any time,
        anywhere, especially in dive-bar restrooms, at abandoned
building sites, and under the table at church bingo games,
        c) English is a simple country girl, but all those words
like elixir, mockingbird, and greengage make her seem
        Mata-Hari mysterious, d) English doesn't give a flying fig
what you think, e) all of the above, because you love
        your capitalist pigs, English, your rape-and-pillage

Robber baron scumbags, your sham millionaire hotel magnate
        turned leader of the Free World, your Waffle-House index
storm damage reports, and while the redwoods burn and Miami burbles
        back into the ocean, English, you are at mission control with interns
who finished high school by the skin of their teeth, and like Chernobyl
        you are testing the system but can't fathom that the cheap

Sleaze-meisters in charge have cut so many corners that we're in Origami
        Land, an amusement park so full of folds it has almost disappeared,
and I don't know about you, but I want a double-fuzz burger on rye
        or maybe a grilled lint sandwich with my 36-ounce kerosene
mocha frappe, because that's all that's on the menu, brothers
        and sisters, and while we're making up words let's not forget

To toast the double-plus-good dose of free will that plays
        to the masses, with their five-hundred-word-vocabulary
urban myths—*Oh honey, everyone says you're a werewolf.*
        The better to eat you, my love. So now I'm Little Red
Riding Hood, and all I wanted was to be Alice drifting on the river,
        but look who's rowing—it's Simon Legree in holey

Underwear, but maybe it's "h-o-l-y," and that's English for you,
        change one or two letters and a pervert turns into a saint,
a priest becomes a pest, a mommy a mummy, a dummy a whammy,
        a Machiavellian-game-show-trumpet mouthpiece turns
into Humpty-Dumpty, a chump, a champ, a chimp with his mouth
        open waiting for the peanuts to fly in his direction,
so have a beer and watch California burn on your TV screen—
        it's The Greatest Show on Earth with a dollop
PeeWee's Big Adventure. Whoa, what's this I see—Visigoths and

Vandals shooting up the back yard with those AK-47's again. No problem,
        baby, because we believe in the transmigration of souls,
an ectoplasmic manifestation of who knows what? Well, here
        we are, English, with front row seats on Mr. Toad's

Wild Ride, careening down the 21ˢᵗ century open road, fueled
        by CBD and craft beers. In case you haven't noticed
this is not Proust's Paris, but wait—maybe it is, because at the end,
        crass, social climbing Mme. Verdurin becomes *La Princesse*
de Guermantes, and isn't that the oldest story in the book?
        What book? And my mother comes back on the river
of souls, and says, *There's only one book, darling, the Bible,*
        and it will tell you everything you need to know, and though
I don't completely agree with her, the Bible has a lot of great stories—
        Adam and Steve, Noah shagging his daughters, Jehovah's

X-ray vision ripping the skin off stinking sinners and sending
       them straight to hell. Anyway, that's where we are, amigos,
treading water in the River Styx, six sheets to the wind, speaking
       English, and trying to figure out what the hell's going on,
but it's hard when English is always changing, I'm talking about hijabs,
       blow jobs, Steve Jobs, not to mention corn-on-the-cob,

Yule logs, eggnogs, and all the Christmas fandango, *oy vey iz mir,*
       OMG, and FYI I'm boycotting the holidays this year
because I just want to lie back, drink Manhattans, eat little snacks
       or *pupus* as the Hawaiians have it, and think about the various
theories in the air, the nutty ones and the esoteric, so baking
       and decorating take up way too much time, and this is our

Zeitgeist, English, Madame Blavatsky to the stars, space alien
       of my inner brain, my dearest mumbojumbologist,
what I love about you is you'll say anything, and God knows you do,
       which makes me want to dig out my brain with scissors,
but here we are in another year at another party in a dark room,
       wrapped in each other's arms, slow-dancing to a love song,
a deep drum, rumble-to-the-core, full carnal score, and you
       whispering in my ear delirious lyrics written just for me.

WHY THE ODE?

I came to the ode through Keats and Neruda. I have always adored Keats's musical lines, and I love Neruda's praise of the ordinary. My first sequence of odes appeared in my second book, *The Alphabet of Desire,* but I was writing them before I began to call them odes.

The ode is often defined as a poem of praise on an exalted subject, but even in the first poems found on cuneiform tablets, which temple poets wrote in ancient Sumeria praising gods, goddesses, and kings, there was a subversive negotiation going on between the poet and the deity. This is also true of the Hebrew Psalms that so influenced Whitman and Ginsberg. They are involved in a complicated kind of praise. Jehovah is a beneficent deity, but he also has a lot of rules and a nasty temper when they are broken.

Nearly two thousand years after the poems of praise by the Sumerian temple priestess Enheduanna, Pindar was writing odes for the victors of the Greek games at Olympia, Nemea, Corinth, and Delphi. And four hundred years after Pindar, in the work of Horace the ode became a more intimate examination of human consciousness in both its public and private masks. Horace also wrote a lot of party odes, which I love, and they come from an even more ancient Greek tradition of having fun in the certain knowledge of our mortality.

The English Romantic poets took the ode and made it a palimpsest of consciousness. Wordsworth, Coleridge, Shelley, and Keats all wrote odes that are still breaking our hearts today. Then in the 1950s the great Chilean poet Pablo Neruda wrote his *Odas elementales* and changed the ode forever with his short lines and praise of such ordinary subjects as the tomato and his socks. The great

Spanish poet Federico García Lorca took the Arabian ode or qasida and made it his own.

Is the ode a form? While an ode can have a specific form, as in Pindar and Horace, it seems to me more of a poetic stance, a poetic investigation of what it means to be a human being at any moment in time. Odes seem to say—*the world is beautiful, but it's terrible, too. Living is a crazy adventure, and then poof it's over.* Unlike the elegy that focuses on the end of lives, the ode celebrates and contemplates living, but, of course, that means keeping an eye on the final curtain as well, so there's an elegiac subtext in every ode.

After writing my first odes, I couldn't stop, and I wanted to know more. What is this human need to praise? What are its motives? The Romantics used the odes to question human mortality. Walt Whitman in his great ode, "Song of Myself," gave voice to the eternal tension between mortality and immortality, and Allen Ginsberg took up the ode as he unlaced the social corset of 1950s America.

And the ode is still being written. There is Bernadette Mayer's "Ode to My Period," Yusef Komunyakaa's sublime "Ode to the Maggot," as well as Kenneth Koch's autobiography in odes, *New Addresses* (2000). Sharon Olds published her *Odes* in 2014, both a beautiful book of praise for the female body and an investigation of aging. So, the ode seems to be without end, a public exclamation of our most private thoughts. It praises, yes, but it asks hard questions and embraces Lorca's duende. From the very beginning of consciousness and its expression in language and writing, the ode has been with us, forging a connection between the world inside us and the beautiful and terrifying one outside.

ACKNOWLEDGMENTS

Many thanks to the editors of the publications where these poems previously appeared, some in different forms:

Action/Spectacle: "Ode to Words for the Body" and "Ode to Juno, Queen of Heaven"; *American Poetry Review*: "Ode to English, Amok and Running," "Ode to My Burning," "Ode on My Mother's Scissors," "Ode to the Lost House," "Ode to the Last Kiss in Venice," and "Ode on Empty Lots and the Devils in the Bushes"; *Delta Poetry Review*: "Ode to my Unquiet Mind in the Bowling Alley of my Soul," "Ode on Conversation," "Ode to My Brother Who I Haven't Spoken to in Thirteen Years," "Ode to the Radio," and "Ode on Junk"; *National Poetry Review*: "Ode in which Athena Tells Off Aphrodite at the Steak and Shake on Jackson Bluff Road"; *The New Yorker*: "Ode on Luck"; *Ploughshares*: "Ode on All My Late-Night Great Ideas"; *Plume*: "Ode on Being a Little Drunk at Parties" and "Ode on the Rilke Metro Stop in the Paris of My Dreams"; *Rattle*: "Box Ode"; *Sixth Finch*: "Ode on *Paradis* and the Longing for a Place that Never Was"; *Smartish Pace*: "Rage Ode" and "Ode for the End of the Party."

"Rage Ode" was inspired by "Rapper's Delight" by Sugar Hill Gang. The opening line, the rhythms, the rhymes, and the humor ignited this poem in my mind.

Stacey Harwood posted a photo of one of her old kitchens on Facebook and a flood of images came rushing out. "Ode to My Old Kitchens" would not exist without Stacey and our love of cooking, especially mushrooms. This poem is dedicated to her.

I don't know what I'd do without my sister, Quincie, who is such an extraordinary artist and all around incredible human being. How lucky am I that she showed up in my world when I was four years old with her sass, smarts, and joie de vivre. There is no one I love to talk story with more than her. I'm so grateful that she lives right down the street from me. How did that happen, *sista*? I don't know, but I'm so glad it did.

Thank you to the amazing poet Susan Wood for reading this manuscript in an early stage and giving me great advice. Thanks also to the editors at Pitt: Nancy Krygowski, Terrance Hayes, Jeffrey McDaniel, and Alex Wolfe. And thanks to Ed Ochester for his support for my work and that of so many others.

I can never express my total adoration and gratitude to David Kirby, for being the best reader, most intrepid travel companion and crazily inventive poet. You make every day a dream come true with your kindness, intelligence, and reportage of weird facts and ideas. As I've said before, I can plan a trip, but you make it fun. The same could be said about our life every day with our darling Patsy and her feral swain Rollo.

There is no greater joy than to pass on your knowledge to students and in turn to learn from them. I could go back thirty years, but right now I'm thinking of Olivia Sokolowski, Bertha Crombet, Alexa Doran, Dorsey Olbrich, Brett Handley, Hayley Laningham, Tacey Attsity, Olga Mexina, Kyle Flak, Chloe Rodriguez, Ifeoluwa Ayandele, Natalie Tombasco, Dallas Saylor, Iain Grinbergs, Natalie Patterson, Sophia Upshaw, Larissa Martins, and Oliver Brooks. Thank you for your youth and your slang.

This book is dedicated to the memory of Stuart Riordan (1950–2022). I first met Stuart through her work. She was sharing a studio with a friend, and I saw an etching of a woman ironing in the heat. You could feel her weariness. The etching was lying on the floor with other papers. When I asked my friend about it, he said, "I think she's going to throw it away." I couldn't believe anyone would throw away something so beautiful. "Ask her if I can have it," I said. He did, and she said yes, but we still hadn't met. When we did meet, we hit it off, and I bought another early etching of her daughter sleeping.

When my first book came out, I asked her to take some photographs for the cover. "Only if you get naked," she said. "No way," I said, but she sweet-talked me into wearing a filmy gown and getting into a pool of water. I might as well have been naked. The resulting cover had a terrible design, but the photograph was beautiful. This led to a series of collaborations through the years, some funded by grants, and other paintings on the covers of subsequent books. One of my favorites was the cover of *On the Street of Divine Love: New and Selected Poems* that features a girl in a party dress being ejected from a car far below. Stuart called me and asked if I had a poem about a car. I sent my poem "Mambo Cadillac" to her, and she copied the poem into the sky above the girl's head. Since "Mambo Cadillac" was in the book, it seemed to be the perfect cover.

Over the years we had many wide-ranging conversations about art and poetry, one of the highlights being when she and her husband Jeff Duvall visited Paris while David and I were living there in 1998. We went to the Louvre one Wednesday evening and happened upon the giant murals that Rubens painted for Marie de Medici. David and Jeff went off to see something else, and I was left with Stuart explaining Rubens genius to me, especially his use of color. It was absolute magic.

Stuart had a beautiful mind, and even when it began to betray her at the end of her life, she retained her joy and optimism. It was such a privilege to be her a friend.